SUPER CUTE!

Baby
Hippos

by Megan Borgert-Spaniol

BLASTOFF!
READERS

BELLWETHER MEDIA • MINNEAPOLIS, MN

Note to Librarians, Teachers, and Parents:

Blastoff! Readers are carefully developed by literacy experts and combine standards-based content with developmentally appropriate text.

Level 1 provides the most support through repetition of high-frequency words, light text, predictable sentence patterns, and strong visual support.

Level 2 offers early readers a bit more challenge through varied simple sentences, increased text load, and less repetition of high-frequency words.

Level 3 advances early-fluent readers toward fluency through increased text and concept load, less reliance on visuals, longer sentences, and more literary language.

Level 4 builds reading stamina by providing more text per page, increased use of punctuation, greater variation in sentence patterns, and increasingly challenging vocabulary.

Level 5 encourages children to move from "learning to read" to "reading to learn" by providing even more text, varied writing styles, and less familiar topics.

Whichever book is right for your reader, Blastoff! Readers are the perfect books to build confidence and encourage a love of reading that will last a lifetime!

This edition first published in 2016 by Bellwether Media, Inc.

No part of this publication may be reproduced in whole or in part without written permission of the publisher. For information regarding permission, write to Bellwether Media, Inc., Attention: Permissions Department, 5357 Penn Avenue South, Minneapolis, MN 55419.

Library of Congress Cataloging-in-Publication Data

Borgert-Spaniol, Megan, 1989- author.
  Baby Hippos / by Megan Borgert-Spaniol.
    pages cm. – (Blastoff! Readers. Super Cute!)
  Summary: "Developed by literacy experts for students in kindergarten through grade three, this book introduces baby hippos to young readers through leveled text and related photos"– Provided by publisher.
  Audience: Ages 5-8
  Audience: K to grade 3
  Includes bibliographical references and index.
  ISBN 978-1-62617-218-0 (hardcover: alk. paper)
  1. Hippopotamidae–Infancy–Juvenile literature. I. Title. II. Series: Blastoff! readers. 1, Super cute!
  QL737.U57B67 2016
  599.63'5–dc23
                    2015009722

Printed in the United States of America, North Mankato, MN.

Table of Contents

Hippo Calf!

A baby hippo is called a calf. It can weigh up to 100 pounds (45 kilograms).

Often a calf is born underwater. Mom pushes it to the **surface** to breathe.

Bonding With Mom

A **newborn** calf **bonds** with its mom. They **nuzzle** to show love.

The calf drinks mom's milk. Eventually it can eat grass.

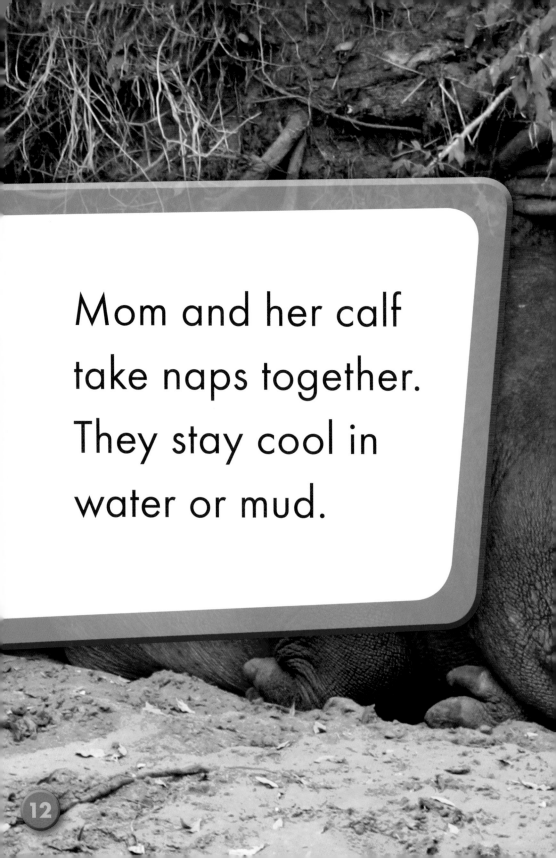

Mom and her calf take naps together. They stay cool in water or mud.

Moving in Water

They also move underwater. The calf can hold its breath for about 40 seconds.

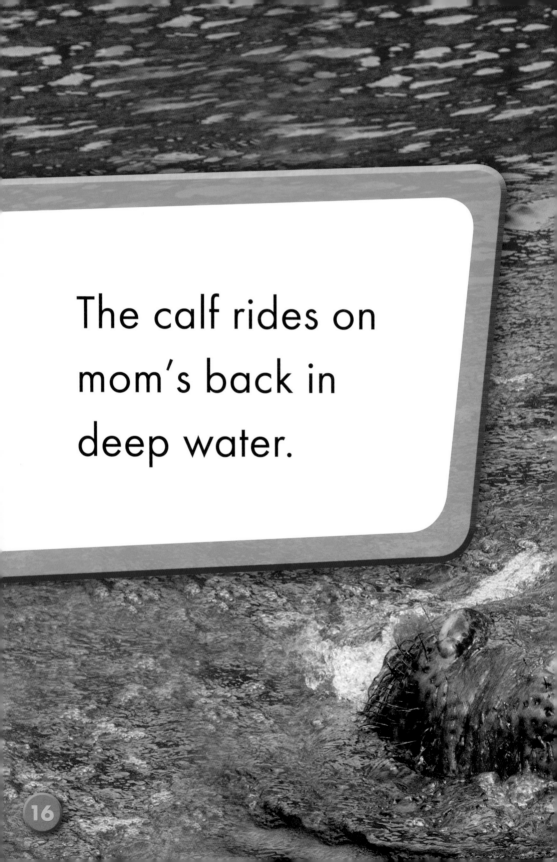

The calf rides on mom's back in deep water.

Joining the Herd

Mom and her calf join the **herd** after one or two weeks.

Adults in the herd watch for crocodiles and other **predators**. Stay close, calf!

Glossary

bonds–becomes close

herd–a group of hippos that live together

newborn–just recently born

nuzzle–to softly rub up against each other with the nose or forehead

predators–animals that hunt other animals for food

surface–the top of the water

To Learn More

AT THE LIBRARY

DiSiena, Laura Lyn. *Hippos Can't Swim: And Other Fun Facts*. New York, N.Y.: Little Simon, 2014.

London, Jonathan. *Hippos Are Huge!* Somerville, Mass.: Candlewick Press, 2015.

Schuetz, Kari. *Hippopotamuses*. Minneapolis, Minn.: Bellwether Media, 2012.

ON THE WEB

Learning more about hippos is as easy as 1, 2, 3.

1. Go to www.factsurfer.com.

2. Enter "hippos" into the search box.

3. Click the "Surf" button and you will see a list of related web sites.

With factsurfer.com, finding more information is just a click away.

Index

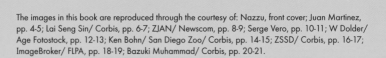